**Birth
is More Than Once**

# BIRTH IS MORE THAN ONCE:

## The Inner World of Adopted Korean Children

Hei Sook Park Wilkinson, Ph.D.

SUNRISE VENTURES
708 Parkman Drive
Bloomfield Hills, MI 48013

Copyright © 1985 by Hei Sook Wilkinson

First Printing, September 1985
Second Printing, April 1986

*All rights reserved,* including the right to reproduce this book, or portions thereof, in any form, except for the inclusion of brief quotations in a review. All inquiries should be addressed to Sunrise Ventures, 708 Parkman Drive, Bloomfield Hills, Michigan 48013.

Library of Congress Catalog Card Number 85-62489

ISBN 0-9615674-0-6

The author would like to thank W. Robert Miller for his permission to use the line "Birth is More Than Once" from his book *Short Footsteps on a Long Journey.*

Cover design by Greg Payea

Printed by Harlo Press, 50 Victor, Detroit, Michigan 48203

# Contents

Acknowledgments   7

Preface   9

1. CONCEPTION: MY OWN EXPERIENCE   13
2. PROCESS   19
   The Children   19
   The Playroom   25
3. THE INNER WORLD OF ADOPTED KOREAN CHILDREN   29
   Being Korean in America   29
      Our relationship   30
      Hey, Chinese!   34
      Feelings about themselves   35
      Language skills   36
   Being Adopted   37
      Children's perception   38
      Fantasies about biological parents   40
      Sibling relationships   42
      Becoming an American citizen   43
   Being Accepted   46
      Nurturing   46
      Trust   50
      Acceptance   52
   Synthesis   53
4. BIRTH IS MORE THAN ONCE: PERSPECTIVES AND IMPLICATIONS   57

Epilogue   65

Bibliography   67

# Acknowledgments

Many warm, caring and deft hands made the birth of this book possible. My profound gratitude extends to Drs. Clark Moustakas, Cereta Perry, and Stanley Krippner, the members of my doctoral committee, who offered me their wisdom, knowledge, and warmth unsparingly. Special thanks are due to Dr. William and Nancy Kiefer, Michael Hall, and Nancy Fox for their careful editing of this book. I am especially grateful to the eight children and their families who made my original study possible with their firm commitment and unmatched enthusiasm. This book is dedicated to them, to my husband, Todd, and my children, TJ and Gina.

# Preface

The material in this book originates from my doctoral research, a phenomenological investigation of the inner world of adopted Korean children. Since the completion of my doctoral degree in psychology, I have had numerous opportunities to share the findings of my research with adoption workers and adoptive parents. Many of them have encouraged me to put the dissertation into book form and make it readily available.

What is not included in this book, but can be found in the original dissertation, are the psychological, scientific and philosophical foundations of the research and the review of relevant literature. Those who wish to review or learn about these foundations can order a copy of the manuscript from Microfilms International in Ann Arbor, Michigan.

This book sheds light on the inner world of Korean children adopted by Caucasian families in the United States. It is intended to provide the children's view of their world. My experiences with them furnished me with many insights. I learned about the special meaning of physical differences and why being teased or ridiculed becomes a crisis. I came to understand behaviors such as the tendency to overeat, to hoard food, to refuse to speak Korean, to shun other Koreans, and to be extremely conforming. I also found the significance of the tension generated by the words "Korea" and "Korean." It is my hope that this book will help parents, adoption specialists and other helping professionals understand the often invisible inner world of adopted Korean children.

# Birth is More Than Once

# 1. Conception: My Own Experience

My interest and involvement in children living under exceptional circumstances began during my high school years in Seoul, Korea. The school had been founded by an American missionary, and each Christian event—Easter, Thanksgiving, and Christmas—was marked with a special ceremony. The Easter of my 16th year was a special one because I debuted as a school choir member. After the ceremony, the choir members had an opportunity to visit an orphanage. We took colorful Easter eggs, our music, and, most importantly, our spirit of celebration. We travelled in an uncomfortable school bus for almost an hour, during which I found myself feeling anxious about the visit. Up to this time, I had had no contact with orphans, let alone an interest in social causes. The bus passed through the main section of the city and into a neighborhood I had never visited. I noticed the worn walls and tile roofs of the houses; the road was badly paved. Finally, the bus stopped at the top of a hill. The director of the orphanage greeted us warmly and led us to the main hall in the orphanage, which later I learned was the dining room.

The children were already assembled in the hall. Small rubber shoes crowded its entrance way. While taking off my own shoes, I caught a glimpse of 50 or 60 children sitting silently on a cold wooden floor. They seemed very well mannered and waited patiently for us to start our program. What impressed me most about these children was their seeming lifelessness. Their faces appeared passive, uninterested, virtually bland. This is reminiscent of the marasmus phenomenon in which infants, who fail to receive warm, personal attention, as well as physical stimulation, tend to become lethargic and apathetic.

As soon as the Easter egg hunt was announced though, their attitude changed into sudden eagerness. I sensed that they perceived it as a fun activitiy but also an opportunity to obtain extra food. We hid the Easter eggs and asked the children to find them. Even before the initial instructions were over, the children began milling around the exit, jostling for position. Later on, many fights broke out between the winners and losers.

In return for our presentation and entertainment, the staff and children of the orphanage had prepared a program for us. A child arose from the first row and stood in the front with folded hands, waiting for a cue. She seemed well rehearsed. As soon as she started singing, I knew I would not enjoy her presentation. Her lifeless voice, her blank face with downcast eyes, and everything else about her evoked sadness in me. I was deeply touched by her presence. I cried silently while listening to her plaintive singing. I noticed other choir members blowing their noses discreetly. At that very moment, I promised myself that I would make some contribution to the lives of these children.

For three years I worked on a regular basis with these children as a volunteer. Often, the orphanage was short of food, clothing, and staff. It seemed to me that the children were constantly hungry for food, love, and warm, human contacts. As a result of my involvement, it became a tradition among students from my high school to devote some of their Sundays to these children.

About 15 years later, I met a man in Detroit who had adopted an eight-year-old Korean boy. He described his son's refusal to talk about his past life in Korea, and his own difficulty and bewilderment in understanding this behavior. To help his son feel more at home, the father had eagerly pointed out events related to Korea from television, newspapers, or magazines. The boy refused to pay attention to these materials and denied prior knowledge about Korea, its language, and its culture. Listening to this, I pondered what was going through the boy's mind. I wondered what it was like for him to be brought to America as the adopted child of an American family. Eventually my curiosity led me into various readings. Most of the research literature focused on characteristics of adoptive parents, initial adjustment of adopted children, and evaluative studies of placements based on statistical analyses of questionnaire data. However, I wanted to discover the meaning of the experience of being a foreign-born adopted child.

The subsequent search to know that inner world rekindled memories from my own life. I was uprooted twice, the first of these involuntarily, and the second, by choice. I was three years of age when the Korean War broke out. My family was told to move from Seoul to Pusan, in the southern part of Korea. We fled Seoul, leaving all our belongings behind. My father was inducted into the army, and my grandfather, as a civil servant, became the main source of income for our family. Amid the confusion and fear that attended the war, I felt like an abandoned child. Many times, when the planes flew over us, I felt alone and unprotected. I was afraid that a plane would bomb us and that no one would rescue us. This fear of abandonment was so overwhelming, I repressed it totally for 30 years. When I finally allowed myself to reexperience this fear, tears streamed down my face, and I screamed in a manner resembling the hollow sound of a fearful child clinging to the warm body of her mother. This reexperiencing became possible as a result of my long, inner search for the meaning of being a Korean woman living in America.

The second incident occurred at the age of 22, when I came to America as a Korean language instructor for the Peace Corps. The initial cultural shock lasted for two or three years. During this transition period, I had to adjust to a completely different life-style—values, customs, foods, and language. I tended to avoid stress and anxiety by keeping myself constantly busy. I would plan events in such a way that I would have to hurry from one place to the other. When I had spare time to reflect upon my life, invariably, feelings of loneliness would engulf me. At those times, nothing and no one could console me. I would sit in my room for hours, just weeping, thinking of my family, friends, the aroma of familiar spices, and the warmth I felt from intimate relationships. Sometimes this feeling of loneliness was evoked by small disappointments or by self-pity, but at other times, by no identifiable reason. It seemed as if a series of massive waves was hitting me hard, without warning. Although I continued to cherish the values, habits, and ways of thinking that I learned from childhood, they were being insidiously eroded. Before I was aware of what had happened, I was being criticized by other Koreans for being "too Americanized." I felt condemned, although I knew a core part of me held onto my Korean identity. However, I began to refer to Koreans as "they" or "them." Yet, I did not feel that I was a member of American society either. I was desperately seeking a group with which to identify and did everything I could to be accepted into American culture.

Years later, when I went back to visit my family in Korea, I found myself afraid of being rejected. I dreaded that I might not remember Korean colloquial expressions or that I might act differently from Koreans. The fear of rejection was so real and terrifying that I stayed up all night in Tokyo wondering how I would greet my family at the airport the next morning. Of course, the new Americanized part of me wanted to embrace each one of my family members, to display my overwhelming excitement and happiness to be with them, but the old Korean part of me was saying "but you cannot behave that way. That is not an acceptable Korean greeting." I was too tired to resolve this dilemma before the plane landed in the Seoul airport. As soon as I walked into the customs area, I spotted my father inspecting each person intently for fear that he might miss his own daughter. When our eyes met, we started running toward each other, and we embraced before I knew what was happening. Nobody seemed to pay attention to us except my father's colleagues at the Customs Office who stood around us with broad smiles on their faces. And my language facility returned in two or three hours as if I had never left Korea. They had accepted me in spite of the changes that I had made. My feeling of family closeness was immediately renewed.

All my life in Korea, except for two or three years after the war, my family—paternal grandparents, parents, and siblings—lived under one roof. Korea, as a Confucian society, expected the oldest son to be responsible for the welfare of his parents. My father was my grandparents' only son; therefore, it was his duty to look after them. They became inseparable parts of my family. As a family unit, we experienced many difficult moments, but, throughout all those times, we were together symbolically, if not physically. There were always people in our home. Each person's role was clearly defined, according to Confucian ethics: "(1) The ruler is the mainstay of the state. (2) The father is the mainstay of the son. (3) The husband is the mainstay of the wife." (Crane, 1967, p.4) I developed a sense of security, rooted in the trust, faith, and intimacy of family members. This sense of security was considerably shaken during my transition period in the United States. Only after I found security within myself, was I able to reexperience my childhood security.

Out of my own experience of displacement, I realized how confused adopted children must be. Koreans had relegated them to the status of nonpersons because they lacked a family, the important basic ingredient of the society. Many of these children were abandoned on the streets at early ages and institutionalized in orphanages and foster homes. The empathy I had for these children and their life experiences, attracted me to the Korean adopted children and, eventually, to the investigation of their inner world. This pursuit was not just a scholastic demonstration but a realization of my long-standing promise to those children with whom I had worked in my high school days.

# 2. Process

### THE CHILDREN

My efforts in locating suitable children for my research were thwarted until I learned of the Intercountry Adoption Services within the Michigan Department of Social Services. This program was initiated in 1976 to fill the demand for home studies in foreign adoption cases, as mandated by Act 237, Michigan Public Acts of 1975. With the help, encouragement, and enthusiasm of its staff, I made contact in 1977 with families in the Detroit tri-county area, (Wayne, Macomb, and Oakland). These families had a Korean adopted child between the ages of four and eight. Eleven such families were interested enough to attend a meeting at which I presented my proposal. To participate in this project, each family was asked to bring their child weekly, for a period of eight months, to a Detroit downtown location. Travel time would be at least 20 minutes one way from their home, and often much further. How their children might be affected was discussed at this first meeting, but no promise of any benefit was made. Eight families enthusiastically committed themselves to the project. The names of these children are changed to protect their privacy.

*Chol-soo*

Nobody knows Chol-soo's exact birthday because he was found abandoned when he was about three weeks old. He was placed in a foster home in Korea and remained there until his adoption by a Michigan couple. He was about five months of age then, the youngest age of adoption among my participants. When I first met him, Chol-soo was four years old, attending a nursery school. Even though his features and size were unmistakably Korean, he impressed me as a typical American boy in his gestures, his mannerisms, and, most of all, his command of English. His capacity for self-expression and his perceptiveness were precocious for a four year old. He helped me, early in my project, to dispel any preconceived notions I might have held about four year olds, and to accept him as an individual. I soon became one of his best "friends." He unhesitatingly shared aspects of his life with me: watching the morning glories he planted climb up a mail box and mature into full blossoms; discovering various designs on paper towels created by the drips from a water faucet; and collecting rubber bands and bobby pins for his soon-to-be adopted sister. His ability to see the world around him with unjaded eyes brought uniqueness to everything he touched in our shared world.

*Young-il*

To Young-il, taking the key and unlocking the playroom were very important activities. He succeeded in opening it everytime, and at those moments, a proud, satisfied smile would appear on his face. He was an albino attending a special education class for the visually impaired. Blonde—nearly white—hair, as well as impaired vision, accompanied the condition, even though he was a full Korean. Like Chol-soo, Young-il did not know his exact age. Different reports varied by as much as two years but he was introduced to me as a seven year old. His physical size fitted this age, but his facial expressions gave him a more mature appearance. As was common in such a situation, he and his parents had to decide what age to put on his permanent record.

Young-il impressed me as a survivor. He appeared to have learned to adapt to institutional life; he knew the feeling of contempt and scorn for his status in Korean society. His determination to survive and his will to live seemed to have hardened him at a young age.

In the beginning of our relationship, he seldom risked revealing his real feelings. Laughter, many times inappropriate, had replaced his pain, fear, and anger. It was a long time before he began trusting me or his family. When pushed or hurried, he would withdraw into a shell, as though frightened by feeling vulnerable. The family's long and tenacious battle to instill in him a sense of belonging, gradually initiated positive changes. Early in our encounter, I sensed his intelligence and common sense. Later, when he relaxed the hardened facade, he was delightful.

## Soon-ja

According to her record, Soon-ja was also abandoned, in an open market place in Korea, before she reached her first birthday. She was temporarily placed in a home for foundlings, and then in a foster home, before she was adopted into a Michigan family at the approximate age of 18 months. She was a pretty, proud kindergarten pupil when I met her. Her petite quality added charm to her well-groomed and sophisticated appearance. To me, she was the prototype of a little lady-child.

As our relationship grew, she began revealing herself. Many moments of joy, confrontation, anger, and sadness were shared, but one recurrent and important issue, was her ambivalence about growing up. Being in kindergarten meant just that—having to grow up. She took much pride in being a "big girl" at school, in following the teacher's instructions, and in doing well in assigned work. She was proud of many newly acquired skills and knowledge, yet she wanted to remain a "baby." She brought her confusion and conflict to our playroom, where she could be what she needed, without being judged. She would appear in lady-like, impeccable dress with the matching socks and purse, and, at times, wearing perfume. When she decided to play an infantile role, she would babble, crawl on the floor, and ask to be fed out of a bottle. There were other times when she would feed herself, playing the roles of both mother and child. She seemed most at peace when she was able to integrate these two roles in her play. Her nurturing self was reflected in her tender care for the imaginary baby.

## Young-hee

Young-hee's adoption record shows that she was also

abandoned at a young age. A foundling home was her only world until she became the adoptive daughter of a Michigan couple at three years of age. She had been a member of that family for two years when I met her. She seemed quite attached to her mother. Even though she was willing to spend time with me in play therapy, she initially appeared unsure of the situation. She walked around me, almost on tiptoes, as quietly as she could. She smiled easily and exhibited friendliness. I sensed, however, that something was lacking in our relationship: for some reason, she was holding back.

For a while, Young-hee felt comfortable sharing only her fragility and infantile tenderness. She selected one place in the playroom and usually stayed in that area, afraid to venture out into unfamliar territory. She asked permission to engage in each activity, but, underneath the politeness, one could observe her insecurity and uncertainty. As she became more trusting of me, an increased self-confidence gradually became evident. Her infantile high-pitched voice and waddling posture started to disappear. She stopped asking for permission prior to undertaking a new activity. She took risks, venturing into those areas of the playroom she had not frequented. She became more willing to share her life with me spontaneously. She started to attend her preschool class at this point, and her mother reported that Young-hee was doing "well," enjoying her school. Young-hee reminded me of a lovely flower ready to bloom.

*Tae-ho*

Tae-ho had been in the United States with his adoptive family for two years when I met him. By that time, he had forgotten most of his Korean and exhibited fluency in his second language, English. Tae-ho also had been abandoned. Even though nobody knew his exact age, he was estimated to be about two and a half years old when found. His adoptive parents thought that he might be about six to twelve months younger than the age given. When I met him, he was almost six, repeating kindergarten. His preschool teacher and the adoption agency had told the parents that Tae-ho was very bright and that he would be able to skip one or more grades. As a result of this prediction, his parents were confused when he had to repeat kindergarten.

My experiences with him in play therapy revealed that, indeed, he was very intelligent. On the surface, he appeared to be spontaneous, friendly, and outgoing, but, right beneath this facade, was an insecure child still not quite sure of his newly acquired world. As the sessions continued and his trust in me grew, he shared many of his feelings of joy and pain concerning his new environment.

*Min-sook*

Min-sook was six and a half years old and in first grade when we began our sessions. Her records indicated that she had been found abandoned at age two in a Korean city hall. She lived in two different orphanages in the next one and a half years, then was brought to the United States for adoption. Three years had passed before I met her. For quite a while, I felt considerable strain in our relationship. She was timid and quiet most of the time. When I extended my words or my hands to reach her, her body stiffened, and high-pitched cries pierced the room. I did not know how to reach her, other than to maintain my distance. She moved about the room tentatively, as if she were afraid to have her presence known. She often complained that the room had unattractive, broken toys, but she always wanted to return.

As she began to feel more at ease with me, and with herself, our relationship often contained spontaneity and sharing. Twenty-seven sessions later, my experience of Min-sook was totally different. She moved around the room without hesitation, and transformed the room into her own world. She took charge, she talked incessantly, and the air was always filled with her laughter and excited shrills. When she selected an activity, she simply immersed herself in it.

*Choon-ku*

Choon-ku was abandoned a few days after birth. Because of poor health, he was hospitalized for the next four months, then placed with a foster family. He was two years and two months old when he was brought to America. According to his foster mother's report, he had only two Korean words in his vocabulary at the time—"umma" (mother) and "pop" (food). It was believed, however, that he understood all of what was said to him. Choon-ku was five when we met.

My first impression of him was that he looked smaller and younger than other Korean boys of his age. During our initial contact, he seldom moved from one place in the playroom to another, and when he did, it was with caution. Even his voice carried shyness and carefulness. I let him set his own pace of contact and exploration. His reticence disappeared as his trust grew. Soon he was able to share his pain, anger, and sadness at being called "Chinese" by other children. He felt hurt, yet he did not have the strength to share this hurt with anybody; the pain was too private and intimate. As he finally became able to share his feelings with me, his play became more varied, spontaneous, and creative; a true expression of his own interests.

*Kyung-ai*

Kyung-ai came to this country from Korea at the age of five. She did not know a word of English at that time, as was true of all other participants in my study. According to her parents, she was very listless, had scars on her face from scabies, scars on her scalp from mites, and an enlarged stomach due to malnutrition. She was extremely uncoordinated and had little energy to engage in activities. When she first arrived in her new home, she needed to stop and rest several times when climbing the steps which led upstairs.

When I met her two and a half years later, she was in first grade and doing well at school. She was shy, avoiding direct eye contact with me. She clung desperately to her father's jacket sleeve. Our relationship began as a threesome—Kyung-ai, her father, and myself. Half way through the first session, her grip relaxed, and she let her father leave the room. From then on, she permitted me some contact, but always at some distance.

To Kyung-ai, fairness was essential. In two-person games, she always checked to be certain that the game began evenly, down to the smallest detail. When we took turns, we had to have the same number of turns, neither more nor less. Her mother reported that this was also true in regard to food at home. If somebody was getting more than his or her share, a loud and disgruntled "HEY!" would escape from her lips, even when her own father began serving himself seconds.

Many times Kyung-ai appeared to be cold and aloof. Often I felt she saw me as an object to be used only when she needed something. She seldom shared her inner feelings with me, and when I expressed mine, her response was a cold, silent stare. This barrier was never completely removed, though she did become more spontaneous in her play.

The children in my study were all full-blooded Korean, between four and seven years of age, had the permission of their parents to participate in the study, and lived in the tri-county area of Detroit, Michigan. All were children who had some awareness of their adoption and of their country of origin, and all were willing to enter into a play therapy setting.

Of the eight children, four male and four female, the average age was 5.9 years. Their mean age at the time of adoption was 3.3 years with 2.6 years of average length of stay in the United States. All the children in my study were more fluent in and comfortable with English than Korean. Therefore, English was used predominantly. Korean was used on rare occasions with one child, whose knowledge of Korean was intact, and then only at his request. All the parents of the eight children were Caucasian. Further, all the children were regarded by their adoption workers as having made a satisfactory adjustment to their new surroundings.

## THE PLAYROOM

The playroom was designed specifically for play therapy. It was chosen for my study mainly for its availability and central location, since the participating families lived in a three-county area around Detroit. The playroom was located in the basement level of a building where there was little traffic. The only way one could identify this room was by the number on the wooden door. The room automatically locked from the outside to insure privacy. It was fairly large, with enough room to allow for physical movement. There were no windows except for a one-way mirror; the observation room behind the one-way mirror was for purposes of training graduate students in psychology. I did not use this room for that purpose, but at times, the children asked to go in the training area and explore. In that sense, it added an extra dimension to our environment.

Directly beneath the one-way mirror was a large sandbox. Invariably, there were cars, Indian figures, soldiers, trucks and utensils hidden under the wet sand, or tunnels and sand castles at the other corner. Clearly, the sandbox was an active world, in which children used their imagination expansively. Adjacent to it, was a life-size workbench with short legs. The top of the workbench, by its marks and dents, showed its hard usage and popularity. Underneath the top, was a storage area for wood pieces and nails, along with a hammer, screwdriver, saw, wrench, and other tools. At times one would find pieces in various stages of creation.

An easel was located next to the workbench. Here, many modes of art could be explored through crayons, magic markers, paints, brushes, colored chalks, and drawing papers. Small containers, in which the paint could be mixed were placed at the bottom of the easel. All these materials were intended to promote open, creative expression. The floor of the room was uncarpeted so that spilled paint could be removed easily.

Facing the easel was a sink with running hot and cold water, built low to accommodate children. At times, it was transformed into a center of activity, such as a family kitchen, a lake with boats, or a reservoir of water. Even the ordinary drain could become a source of wonder for some children. They were fascinated with how quickly or slowly the water ran, and experimented with methods to vary the flow. A boxful of play plates, forks, knives, spoons, pots and pans were at their disposal on the counter top of the sink area. Behind the easel was a dartboard mounted on a corkboard. So as not to inhibit inexperienced throwers, the dartboard covered almost the entire height of the wall and one fourth its width.

Small toys and materials were placed on an L-shaped counter, running along the other two walls, and placed at a height suitable for children. The material included a telephone, cash registers, baby milk bottles, a physician's bag, tinker toys, a playhouse-sized wooden bench, several large-sized dolls with an array of clothes, human figures and animals made out of rubber, human and animal hand puppets, books and other playschool material, along with a few small musical instruments. Above and under the counter were blue cabinets storing excess or extra-large materials. When children explored these cabinets, they found various board games, books, miniature wooden furniture for a playhouse, wooden blocks, toy guns and knives, fencing tools, crafts material and extra art supplies.

The bathroom was located in one corner of the playroom, and a small closet in another contained brooms, dustpan, and a mop. "Bobo," a 3 foot-tall inflated punch bag, could be taken to any part of the room. The table and the set of chairs in the middle of the room could be rearranged to suit the needs of a particular session. Last, but not least, was a round clock on a wall which served as a connection to external reality. Children soon learned to plan their time so that they could make the maximum use of the session.

The playroom thus lent itself to unimpeded use by children. Its design encouraged free play, and its diversity stimulated the child's imagination.

# 3. The Inner World of Adopted Korean Children

What is the inner world of adopted Korean children as revealed in play therapy? In our play therapy sessions, the children disclosed their thoughts, dreams, fantasies, and feelings on a wide variety of topics. Play took many forms, including puppet play, music, dialogues, movement, and make-believe. I sifted through the vast amount of data and grouped my findings into three categories: (1) being Korean in America, (2) being adopted, and (3) being accepted.

## BEING KOREAN IN AMERICA

The children in the study had been adopted from Korea by Caucasian Americans, and this fact alone was a significant aspect of their being. All the children had unmistakable Oriental features. Although communication in English was never a real problem, they had noticeable difficulties in pronunciation. The children had been constantly reminded of these differences, sometimes in a positive manner, and sometimes not. Many issues and experiences which the children related to me resonated from their sense of non-being. The children perceived most of their physical and cultural differences from other "Americans" as negative and threatening. At these times, they regarded the world as hostile, and reported feeling alienated. Thus, being Korean was regarded by the children as something less than desirable. The fact that I was Korean seemed to have provoked feelings of insecurity and fear about their past life in

Korea, and possibly a vague threat to their newly attained life. However, as our relationship and mutual trust grew, they began to regard me as a confidante who could understand them more, because of our shared nationality and experiences. Gradually, they dared to reveal their inner selves, and came to a place of equilibrium, while exploring the vital issues of being Korean in a foreign land.

## Our Relationship

I begin by describing how the children related to me, the researcher and the play therapist who was also Korean. Each child had been told in advance, by the parents, that he or she would be seeing a Korean woman who desired to learn about adopted Korean children. After the play therapy sessions began, I spoke no Korean words unless the child requested them. However, references were sometimes made to Korean food, games, songs, and the like, when they were important in sharing my own experiences. Initially, most children had an immediate reaction to me, ranging from deliberate avoidance to quick acknowledgment of our shared nationality.

Tae-ho developed the most extreme reaction of all. During our first session, he spent most of the time exploring the playroom and making contact with me in a most cautious and reserved manner. I learned from his mother that on the way home that day, he did not speak a word to her—which was quite unusual. As soon as he walked into the house, his mother recollected, he "burst into tears and bawled and bawled in a very upset manner." Sensing his insecurity, his parents hugged him and told him many times that they loved him, and that nobody would take him away from them. He was too upset that evening to verbalize what bothered him. The next day, when he felt better, he was able to tell his mother that he had been afraid that I was going to take him out another door of the playroom, that his mother would not see us leave, and that I would take him back to Korea. He said to her, "Sook lives in Korea and has an airplane and goes home to Korea every night." What a nightmare that must have been for him! Thanks to his mother's sensitive and perceptive handling of the matter, Tae-ho recovered, and, surprisingly, even expressed a desire to return to the playroom.

While Tae-ho was cautious and reserved, Min-sook avoided contact entirely. She explored the room in her first two sessions, engaging in a few activities, but avoiding interaction with me. In our third session, when I shared my feelings about being ignored, she began to cry and then to wail loudly. She did not allow me to come near her, touch her, or comfort her. Her body was as stiff as if it were frozen. This behavior continued in the next session. After repeatedly shrieking, however, she eventually quieted down and fixed her gaze on the floor without blinking. The rest of the session was spent in pregnant silence, with Min-sook seemingly glued to one spot, while I was curious, yet allowing her to be. I was puzzled as to what had triggered these events, for my initial approaches to her had been gentle, devoid of harshness or blame. This mystery was solved when Min-sook's mother called me three days after the fourth session. Min-sook had told her parents that she was frightened by me because I was Korean, and that she was afraid of being alone with me in the playroom. She asked her parents what my husband was like and whether I had any children. Her parents thought that Min-sook feared that I was checking her out in order to adopt her myself. Reassurances from her parents allayed her fears, and she entered in a new way the next time I met her.

Soon-ja verbalized the feelings several other children seemed to have. She related that when she first met me she was so "scared" to be with me that she was "shaking to death." She was scared, she said, because she had never talked with a Korean woman before, and she did not know what was going to happen.

Behind their initial apprehension lay a fear of another possible disruption of their lives. I, to them, represented the people of Korea who had interrupted their lives in the past. One way they dealt with this fear was to deny their ethnic background, refusing to identify with me in any way. Initially any mention of Korean food, language, songs, or even the word "Korea" was met with silence or an attempt to change the topic.

As our relationship grew, however, and our mutual trust deepened, this stage of denial ended. Gradually, they asked many personal questions: Do you have a mother and a father? What are their names? Do you have any children? Do you want any babies? Do you have a husband? Is he Korean? What's his name? What do you think about being Korean? Once the questioning was satisfied, statements appeared that enabled us to develop relationships. One day Min-sook chose two identical hand puppets and gave one to me. She held up her puppet and exclaimed to mine, "You look like me. You look like me. You look just like me!" Young-hee once brought an Oriental-looking doll that she had received as a present for her fifth birthday. Showing it to me proudly, she stated, "My doll's name is Sook like yours. She has dark hair like you and me."

Kyung-ai reached a point of identifying herself with me and admitting her Korean origin. Her father reported the following episode:

> While vacationing in Florida she twice pointed out to her parents recognition of other "Koreans." While watching sharks at Marineland, she turned to her Dad and whispered "That man's Korean." We couldn't hear him speaking. Her recognition was apparently physical. She seemed mildly delighted in her discovery and in the fact that she was telling someone else about it—an act we don't recall ever happening before. Several days later at Disney World she said to her mother, "There are sure lots of Koreans here." She now identifies all Asians as Koreans, though we have explained that there are Japanese, Chinese, etc. Again her recognition seemed to carry a tone of pleasant surprise, perhaps as though she hadn't been aware that so many other Orientals were all about us.

Through questioning of me and expressing and relating their own experiences, the children explored the meaning of being Korean and came to accept themselves as Korean. By the end of the research project, most of the children seemed to regard me as a friend. On occasion, they recalled experiences in Korea. They began to make comments like the following:

> "Would you teach me Korean? It doesn't feel good to forget my own language."
> "I'm an American citizen Korean."
> "I'm Korean except I'm American most of the time." or
> "I like being Korean."

Young-il first showed his new-found ability to integrate past and present comfortably in this dialogue:

> YI: Do you have a Korean song? Sing it.
> SW: You want to hear a Korean song.
> YI: Uh huh (nodding).
> SW: (sings Hakkyo Chong-i [school bell])
> YI: (with a grin of acknowledgment) No, not that one.
> SW: Not that one? Which one, then? (pause) (hums Nabi-ya [butterfly])
> YI: (again with a smile) No, not that one.
> SW: (sings Chi-r-rung [bicycle]) Do you know that song?
> YI: Uh huh. (And he joins in the singing, continuing his game of checkers.)

As he moved the checkers, he admitted that he missed Korean food.

In Choon-ku's case, there was a different air about him when he entered the room for our last session. Abruptly, he announced that his original Korean name had been Choon-ku, and that he had been renamed Bob after entering his adoptive family. In his announcement, I sensed a pride and sureness. It seemed to be his way of owning an important component of his past. He was announcing to the world who he was then. This kind of disclosure came as a total surprise since many parents had reported that their children did not remember their Korean names. During play therapy with an adult Korean female, the children experienced a process of finding their Koreanness, repossessing it, and integrating it into their present lives.

## Hey, Chinese!

Being Korean also meant being open to teasing. Most instances that the children reported involved people outside the family, usually other children in school, or in passing. Even though the adoptive parents had told their children that they were Korean, not Chinese, and that being Korean was something they could be proud of, this provided little solace. Choon-ku related: "I feel bad when people call me Chinese. I feel like punching them." He then grabbed a stuffed figure sitting next to him, punched it with a hard fist, and trampled on it angrily. Tae-ho stated: "When I was walking to school, everybody called me Chinese. How would you feel if you were walking to school and someone call you Chinese? How'd you feel if somebody do that to you?" He reasoned out loud that "all Koreans have Chinese eyes," and that "it's dumb to have Chinese eyes even though people don't say it out loud." He suggested calling the teasers "Japanese" as a way to get back at them, but decided not to because he might be "jailed" for saying a bad word.

Soon-ja shared her experience with intense anger, disgust, and irritation.

> SJ: People call me Chinese, Japanese, everything. You know what I call people, if they call me Chinese?
> SW: What?
> SJ: Where are you from, turkey—Turkey?
> SW: You tell them that?
> SJ: No.
> SW: You want to say that to them.
> SJ: Only I can't. You know why?
> SW: Why?
> SJ: I'll get in trouble.

These episodes exemplify several points beyond their sensitivity when teased about their features. Some of the children were not convinced that their Korean heritage was something to be proud of. They were hesitant to defend themselves and afraid of getting into trouble. Just as important, they tended to keep their feelings to themselves. In fact, their parents were surprised to learn of the intensity and depth of these feelings because they were seldom revealed at home.

Kyung-ai was coming to see me when two girls called to her, "Hey! Chinese girl!" as she passed. Her father who was with her at the time, noticed that she was embarassed and that she tried to hurry down the hall. He went on:

> We talked to her about this, and she revealed that a few other kids at school had called her similar names. She had never readily admitted this to us before, and perhaps would not have done so this time except for our inquiring. We explained that all kids get called names, and that she shouldn't pay attention to name callers. We tried to be positive in explaining that we think her eyes are beautiful.

In sharing their experiences with me, I sensed that the children wanted more to release their hurt, angry feelings and have them acknowledged than to learn how to combat their tormentors. Many asked me if I had ever experienced being called Chinese and how I had felt. I shared with them the fact that as an adult I knew intellectually that the children who called me Chinese in a derogatory fashion were rude and did not know any better, but that I also felt hurt and angry. It was comforting for them to learn that others close to them had been subjected to teasing as well.

*Feelings About Themselves*

The children expressed mixed feelings about being the only, or one of the few, Koreans in the immediate world of their family, school, and community. At times, when they regarded their differences negatively, the feelings aroused were sadness and loneliness. Tae-ho was very much aware of these feelings, and was curious about me as well. He asked "Is anybody Korean at your house? Is there somebody next door to you that's Korean?" Hearing that I was the only Korean in my home and neighborhood, he quickly responded, "I am, too." He went on to say that he often felt sad and lonely in being the only Korean in his family. These feelings arose most poignantly when he felt that no one really understood him. Young-hee shared how "bored" she felt when alone. As we delved more deeply into her feelings, she revealed that she felt "bored" when she felt that nobody wanted her. She observed that none of her friends looked like her, and neither did her parents. When she felt that nobody wanted her, she experienced rejection and attributed it to her being different. She felt sad and lonely at those times. When I shared my feelings of loneliness and sadness, her eyes brightened and she asked, "Do you wish you could be with me at those times?" and went on to say "I wish I could be with you for a long time when I'm sad."

Along with sadness and loneliness, children reported moments when they felt positive about being Korean. Minsook spoke proudly of receiving a package from Korea that contained her Christmas gift—a Korean dress. With excitement, she speculated how pretty and unique she would look in it. She stated that she was fortunate to be Korean, for she would be the only one with a Korean costume. She then proceeded to say "I'm going to take the dress to my school. I'll let my friends touch it." Young-il found pride in being able to maneuver chopsticks well. He remarked that he was the only one in his family who could use them with ease. As children shared these feelings of uniqueness and self-esteem, I sensed a harmony and tranquillity in them.

*Language Skills*

Another major theme related to being Korean was language. From my experience with other adopted Korean children and reports from adoptive parents, I learned that the children often are reluctant to speak Korean with other Korean-speaking people. Young-il, whose Korean was still quite intact, preferred to communicate in English with me the majority of the time, even though he knew that I spoke Korean. He made frequent remarks concerning English:

> YI: You know American letters? Would you teach me how to American letter?
> SW: Would I teach you how to write or how to read...?

YI: (even before I finished the sentence) Uh huh, read.
SW: How to read American letters?
YI: Uh huh. (At times, he would correct my English pronunciation and insist that his English was better.)
SW: You like to do things that other kids do.
YI: (quickly) Kids, not kits.
SW: Kids? (not realizing immediately that he was correcting me) Oh, okay.
YI: You're saying it wrong.
SW: You like correcting my English.
YI: Uh huh (nodding his head). You're saying the wrong thing. Wrong sound. That's not right English. Right English. Speak real good English.
SW: And you want to speak real good English.
YI: Yep. Better than you. You don't know how to speak English at all.

Choon-ku was curious to know how I had learned my English, commenting proudly that his mother had taught him. He, like most of the children in the study, had almost completely forgotten Korean. I believe that learning to speak English for Young-il, Choon-ku, and others meant more than communication; it was a means to fuller acculturation and acceptance into American life.

## BEING ADOPTED

Since the children in the study were born to Korean parents in Korea, and were then released or abandoned at various ages, they fantasized about their biological parents, especially their mothers. They did not seem to be interested in actual accounts of what had happened to them except for one gnawing question: Why did she not keep me? They feared a similar rejection by their adoptive families. Through adoption, they began a new life with a new status and new citizenship. They were born again with all the excitement, joy, pain, and struggle that accompany birth, and they were very happy about it. When other Asian adopted children were present in the family, the children felt close to them, possibly due to their similar background as Asian adopted children.

## Children's Perception of Adoption

To most children, adoption meant, first and foremost, gaining a mother and father of their own. Their perception of adoption was concrete. Soon-ja related that adoption meant "somebody comes and picks up their little girl." Chol-soo observed "You send away a lot of papers to get a child." He had astutely observed the process when his parents made efforts to adopt a third child. In Young-hee's perception "People adopt you to love you when your parents are dead because they're too old."

The children's descriptions of their new parents were mostly given in functional terms, seeing them primarily as caretakers. Young-hee stated that "Mother takes care of kids, can do many things, is always busy and likes being that, and gets sick sometimes." When Young-hee thought about possibly losing a mother through death, immediately she came up with a solution: "Then they [the children] would have to have a babysitter to live with them." Kyung-ai often described a mother as "somebody who changes baby's clothes, cooks, makes bed, folds clothes and washes."

However functional were their views of their mother and father, all the children also expressed intense possessiveness of their parents. Young-il, who had been in the United States for less than a year, and was at times quite homesick, asked me if I was planning to go back to Korea or stay in America. I responded that I wanted to go back to visit my family and friends. Immediately, he said, "Not me. I don't have any Mom and Dad. I'm going to stay, cause I have my Mom and Dad here." To him, having and keeping parents was much more important than going back to the land and people he had left behind. He was proud and happy to have his own parents. These feelings were shared by all the children in the study. Soon-ja, for example, made Easter eggs out of Playdoh material. One egg "hatched" but did not have a mother. Soon-ja quickly began making a mother for the chick. When the parent was finally made, Soon-ja impersonated the chick "quacking" in happiness to have a mother. She commented "I never thought the baby'll be so glad of Mom."

The children that I met in play therapy sessions also described a deep-seated fear of separation, fear of being taken away or abandoned. This fear was more pronounced, I believe, because of their previous life experiences. Young-hee, especially at the beginning of the project, frequently speculated about where her mother was while she stayed with me. Intellectually, she knew that her mother sat in the lobby waiting but Young-hee needed to check many times to be reassured. Min-sook frequently expressed her fear of abandonment in her play. For many sessions, she portrayed children who lost their parents, children who wandered off and did not know their way back home, or sometimes children whose mother had intentionally left them behind. As she continued to work on her fear of abandonment in our sessions, she began to find solutions for the lost children. At times, they were met by their parents. At other times, she played store that sold lost and found babies. An excerpt follows:

> MS: What you want? There's the books and here's all the stuff. These are not dolls, these are babies. These are babies (emphatically). This is lost and found.
> SW: They were lost and found?
> MS: By the police.
> SW: Oh, those babies look so pretty.
> MS: You can sell. I want you to be my mommy (pretending to be one of the baby dolls). You got a baby?
> SW: Yes, and I need a brother for the baby.
> MS: (pretending to be another baby) I'm a boy.

As this scene continued, Min-sook lowered one baby's age to make him more adoptable and rejected sick or dirty babies as unadoptable. In a later session, she eventually covered the actual process of being moved from one place to a new family, being given new clothes to wear, being given a new name, and being introduced to a new neighborhood. She even gave tips on how to behave in the new family.

Tae-ho feared he would be sent back to Korea for being bad, which to him meant breaking rules. For instance, he was allowed to watch television at 5:30 p.m., and even when no one was around, he would not turn it on earlier.

> TH: I just sit there and play until 5:30.
> SW: What happens if you watch TV before 5:30?
> TH: And I didn't ask my Mom?
> SW: Uh huh.
> TH: Her be mad!

A short time later he burst out spontaneously, "I hate to go back to Korea." I sensed that this fear underlay a great deal of his adherence to rules. From what they shared during their play, I believe it was a fear felt by many of the other children.

### *Fantasies About Biological Parents*

"Whose tummy did I come out of?" This simple, fundamental question often asked by the children marked the first articulated step into exploring their past. When asked the question, all the parents reportedly told their children that they had been in the "tummy" of a Korean lady who could not keep them. This statement led the children into the next level question, "Why did she not or could she not keep me?"

As Chol-soo's mother related to me, she and Chol-soo had just watched a birthing experience on television. She decided that it was a fortuitous opportunity to remind her son about the meaning of his adoption. She went on to tell him that another mother had carried him in her "tummy" and gave birth to him, but because she could not care for him, he became their "little boy." She continued, "For the first time, he asked why his other mother could not care for him. We talked about the reasons some mothers cannot care for their children—primarily the circumstances of poverty—in terms I thought he could understand."

The gnawing question, "Why did she not keep me?," kindled a series of fantasies in the children in an attempt to satisfy their need to bring some closure to the question. During our sessions, children played out some of these fantasies.

Choon-ku, one day, absorbed himself in making human figures with Lego pieces. He created a father, a mother, and a son figure. Then he opened his drama by sending the father figure away from home. The mother was gravely ill in bed, and the young son was left alone to take care of the mother. During the course of the drama, the mother's illness became progressively worse and the son had to call a hospital. Similar scenes were enacted in later sessions and stopped only when the mother "died." Soon-ja's fantasies often portrayed a family—father, mother, son, and daughter—going on a trip in a toy bus. In one of these, she seated all the family members in the bus, the son next to the father, and the daughter with the mother. Then the bus "accidentally" turned over, killing the mother and the father, leaving the brother and sister alive. Soon-ja gave an elaborate description of the bloody scene, as if she had witnessed it in real life.

Min-sook's fantasies varied, yet all carried the same theme of a child losing her mother. In one, she portrayed a girl whose mother was hospitalized and never came home. In another, she pretended to be a three year old girl wandering in search of her mother. Min-sook described how the girl's clothes were dirty, how she was crying, and how she might die of hunger. And yet another time, a mother and her daughter were on their way to a party. They were already late for the party, and the mother started walking fast, thinking that the daughter was following behind her. Alas, the girl could not catch up and eventually lost her way. Speculating aloud as to why the mother did not keep her "baby," she said, "Maybe mother hated the babies, or maybe she just lost you [a lost baby]."

Like many other children, Young-hee's fantasies centered around portraying herself as incorrigible. One time she dramatized herself as a girl who was angry at her mother. The girl threw a chair at the mother, resulting in the mother's hospitalization and her eventual death.

Some children speculated if their biological parents were still alive and, if so, where they were. Kyung-ai's fantasy was revealed in the following conversation, recorded by her father.

> We continued discussing that Mom and I didn't know anything about her first [Korean] mom and dad, that perhaps they were dead. She agreed, but added that she thought her first mom was very old and that she saw a Korean man at the store one day. He had black hair, was quite tall and had a gray coat on. Her description led me to believe she must have carefully examined his appearance at the time she saw him. I told her that her first dad is probably still in Korea if he's alive. I told her she could ask Sook about Korea, because Sook was already grown up when she came to the United States and would remember lots of things about life there. "Hey, maybe Sook is my first mom!" she said excitedly.

Soon-ja often fantasized the interaction between a mother and her baby girl. The mother made the baby's life miserable. In return, the baby showed her anger by being "bad"—throwing away the food her mother cooked, and doing the opposite of what she was told. Then the mother would spank the baby, or threaten to report her to Daddy. The baby viewed the mother as nagging and demanding.

These fantasies reflected how the children viewed themselves and their biological parents. As they brought closure to one question about their past, new questions arose. I believe that this quest into the past would continue its cycle until the children came to accept living with the unknown.

*Sibling Relationships*

Through adoption, the children gained not only parents but new siblings as well. By coincidence, the four girls in my study all acquired older non-adopted brothers. Reports of occasional competitive feelings and fights were the only suggestions of sibling rivalry.

Each of the four boys in the study became the oldest child in his family. Chol-soo acquired a younger brother adopted from Vietnam, Tae-ho a sister adopted from Michigan, and Choon-ku a sister adopted from Korea. Young-il gained a non-adopted sister and a brother adopted from Vietnam.

Of all the children, Young-il most often expressed intense competitive feelings against his sister. He often compared himself to her. His sister, who had been the only child, confided in me that she did not particularly appreciate losing her "first child" status, either, and thereby resented having an older brother. Young-il clearly conveyed his sensitivity of how his mother treated him in comparison to his sister. On one birthday, he related, "I wanted that Spiderman coloring book. My mother wouldn't let me have it. But she will let my sister have it. Sometimes when I want things, she won't give them to me but she will to my sister." Another time he related: "My brother took away my ChapStick. My sister has three but my Mom wouldn't give me another." He interpreted this as demonstrating that his mother liked him less than the other children in the family, especially his sister.

While his sensitivity was acute in regard to his sister, Young-il's attitude toward his Vietnamese brother was quite different. His attitude was similar to that of Chol-soo and Choon-ku who both had Oriental siblings. They expressed feelings of closeness and protectiveness for their younger siblings, even though, like others, they also occasionally engaged in fighting and bickering. Discussing his adopted sister from Korea, Choon-ku related "I feel sad when somebody hits me, but I feel mad when they hit my sister." Chol-soo made a similar remark: "I get upset with my Mom when she gets upset with my brother." He also talked about how adept he was in "reading little people's mind," like his brother's.

In general, feelings of deep affection and solid connection were more common in discussions of Oriental siblings than of non-adopted ones, especially when close in age.

*Becoming an American Citizen*

During the course of the project, three children were in

the process of becoming American citizens, something people born in this country take for granted. The other children did not meet the naturalization requirement, which existed at that time, of living in this country for three years as permanent residents before applying for citizenship. Those who did, however, expressed apprehension and anxiety about becoming citizens when they were first approached by their parents. To them, the word "citizen" did not have any meaning cognitively, although they sensed that something significant was going to happen. One day Choon-ku heard his mother talking on the telephone. The following is an account of conversation that took place between Choon-ku and his mother, as reported by the mother.

CK: Who are you calling, Mom?
MO: I've called immigration to see if they have the papers I sent them so you can become a citizen.
CK: (defensively) I don't want to be a citizen.
MO: I think you'll be happy to be a citizen when you understand more about it.
CK: Is K [his adopted sister from Korea] going to be a citizen?
MO: Yes, when she's older.
CK: Do citizens live with their mothers and fathers?
MO: Boy and girl citizens do until they want their own home, but they live with their mothers and fathers as long as they want.
CK: (more relaxed) I want to be a citizen.

His parents had been preparing him for the important event that was to come several months later. The evening before the day, during a dinner, Choon-ku opened the conversation. "When do we go to see the man—the one who'll help me become a citizen?" At that the sister who was one and a half years younger asked "Mom, what's a citizen?" The mother answered, "Well, a citizen of the United States is usually someone who lives here. Sometimes citizens are born here. But if you were not born here, you can go to see a judge and you can be a citizen. Then you can help to decide how things will be here. For instance, if two men want to be President, you can vote for one you think should be President." Choon-ku commented, "Well, at first, I will vote for President, then I will be the President." As was demonstrated in the above conversation, Choon-ku's original anxiety over the occasion was replaced with something positive he could anticipate.

Chol-soo was three and a half years old when his parents began citizenship proceedings. At the time of application, his parents also tried to explain to him the meaning of becoming a citizen. They told him: "When you're born in one country and go to live in a new country, you get to be a citizen of the new country." They reminded him that he was born in Korea, but now he lived in the United States, and so he could become a citizen of this country. His mother continued: "Citizens can do special things like voting." Chol-soo listened carefully, then said, "But Mom, what's a citizen?"

A few days later, he was watching a program on senior citizens on television. Suddenly, he became excited, and shouted, "Mom, they're talking about citizens, like me!" At his nursery school, when the teacher asked the children what they wanted to be when they grow up, there were many different answers including Chol-soo's who proudly announced "When I grow up, I'm going to be a citizen." When the day came, he went to the court with his parents, stood next to other aliens, swore the oath of allegiance, and sat through the judge's speech, exhibiting good manners. Afterwards, the parents took him to a restaurant to celebrate the occasion. Chol-soo proudly announced to the manager the important event of the day—"I've got a new puppy and we're having company for dinner tonight." It seems the occasion had far more significance to the parents than to the child himself. What was more important to him was the fact that he received a puppy as a gift.

Soon-ja had just returned from the Immigration Office when the following conversation took place in one of our sessions. She had gone there to have an interview with an immigration officer, the last step of becoming a citizen before the swearing-in.

SW: Are you a citizen now, Soon-ja?
SJ: No. In three months I'm gonna be one.
SW: What does it mean to you to become a citizen?
SJ: I'm gonna be Korean. I'm gonna be an American citizen Korean.
SW: You're still going to be Korean but you'll be an American citizen.
SJ: I'll *always* be Korean (emphatically).

In summary, becoming an American citizen evoked many different responses in the children. To Soon-ja, reaffirming her Koreanness was an important aspect of the occasion. Choon-ku wanted to make sure that as a citizen, he could still live with his parents and sister. To Chol-soo, obtaining a puppy meant more than becoming a citizen itself. These diverse meanings indicate that the personal process experienced by each child needs attention, as well as the long and enduring legal aspects of the naturalization process.

## BEING ACCEPTED

The psychological needs of the children were expressed in their actions during play therapy. The expressions consisted of nonverbal data which were interpreted in the light of the particular context of the moment.

By the time I began working with them, the children had settled into their lives with their adoptive families. Satisfying their basic needs for food, shelter, and clothing was no longer a concern. They did, however, express other needs that seemed to arise from their particular circumstances. The children rarely articulated these needs directly, but often reflected them in their play, as they struggled to hide their vulnerability and to protect themselves from further hurt and frustration.

*Nurturing*

A need for intensive nurturing manifested itself in many forms; most of these revolved around mothering, a wish to be an infant again, and a craving for food. Many children often played the role of either mother or baby, or sometimes both simultaneously. In this way, they could regress to infancy or demonstrate their wish to be nurtured.

Soon-ja frequently engaged in such play. One day, she nurtured a toy dog with extreme tenderness and affection. She lifted the "baby" to her eye level, making affectionate cooing sounds, then held it tightly in her arms, cheeks touching. She pretended to "feed" the "baby" and put it to sleep, patting it gently, then covering it caringly. Another time, while preparing for painting, she noticed a baby bottle and asked about its function. I told her that it was there for play in whatever way she preferred. She decided to wash the bottle and fill it with water. Then she announced that she was Baby Pinky, three years of age. She placed herself in a chair and started sucking, at first with awkwardness, but soon with ease. She then placed herself on the floor, crawling around on her hands and knees, babbling. This theme was repeated in her play for three months. One day, she picked up the baby bottle and began to write her name in the sand by squirting water out of the nipple. That was the final episode of her infantile role-playing. From that point on, her play was that of a typical five-year-old child.

It took Tae-ho four sessions before he permitted himself to imitate an infant. Until then, he had played with the baby bottles, cleaning them, filling them up with water, and pouring the water out of them. Finally, he offered me one of the bottles filled with water and asked me to drink. In silence, I took it and started sucking on the nipple. I believe that this was his way of testing to see if "being a baby" was an acceptable behavior in my presence. Once reassured, he also started drinking out of the bottle, finishing one, and soon grabbing another. He remarked that "the baby is being fed because he is hungry. The baby needs milk." While drinking "milk," he began sharing his feelngs about being Korean, recalling experiences of his early life in Korea.

Kyung-ai accidentally discovered that rocking on the Bobo was soothing to her. On several occasions, she let out the air a bit so that there was enough there to hold her up, yet remain soft and cuddly. She would put the Bobo down on the floor horizontally, lay on it, and gently rock herself back and forth while hugging it. This tacit admission of vulnerability was in direct contrast to her previous guarded behavior.

Food, as a basic need, had been an issue for most of the children in their past. Young-hee acted out this need in one of her family plays. She served food made out of sand and water to imaginary family members. Everybody in the family had small servings except the father. She also gave large portions to herself and to me "because we are big." Then, out loud, she speculated how the children felt about not having enough food. She went on to say that she did not have enough when she was a little baby and remembered how bad she felt, and that she was happy now to have "lots of food in America." It is not uncommon to hear from the adoptive parents that their children consume a great deal of food. Young-il's parents revealed:

> One week after Young-il's arrival was Thanksgiving Day and is honored, in our family, by a large gathering of relatives and an even larger meal...Young-il ate mashed potatoes, turkey, gravy, dressing, cranberry, relish, green beans, sweet potatoes, lima beans, tossed salad, molded jello salad, tomato aspic, nuts, apples, oranges, bananas, ice cream, hard boiled eggs, milk, olives, pickles, spiced apples, carrot sticks, cherry tomatoes, pumpkin and mincemeat pies...Young-il was sound asleep when we got home and his daddy tossed him into bed. I unsnapped his slacks and grabbed his cuffs and tried to take off his pants. I was instantly engulfed in a shower of food— nutmeats and apple pieces in his shorts; hard boiled eggs in his sock tops not to mention his pockets which were stuffed with all manner of goodies.

Having experienced and observed orphanages in Korea myself, I could understand how this boy might have thought that the time had finally come to compensate for extended period of hunger.

At times, food seemed to assume a different significance. From the very beginning of our relationship, Young-hee often asked whether I was going to give her a snack. At first,

I thought that she was expecting what she was used to having in preschool, but when her question persisted, I began to interpret it differently. Its deeper meaning became clear in her play. A stuffed figure which she named Humpty Dumpty was crying. Young-hee made some soup out of sand to comfort him. She then remarked that this five-year-old Humpty Dumpty was happy when food and drink were given to him. She also talked about how important her snack time was in preschool. At Easter time, she brought me a cupcake as a gift. I thanked her and did not pay much further attention to it. During the session, she asked me if I had brought something for her from a grocery store. She kept looking at the cupcake and finally said "You can eat the cupcake now." Since it was early in the morning, I told her that I would eat it at lunch time. Then I realized what she was really asking for. I offered her half of the cupcake and watched her eat it happily. Her contented look indicated that she felt nurtured.

The ritual of preparing and serving food constituted a large part of Young-hee's play. Typically, she would make special foods. One day she celebrated her grandfather's birthday by conjuring up an entire meal—stuffed chicken, ice cream, "fancy" strawberry pie, coffee, and more. She hummed a lullaby joyfully as she performed the make-believe cooking and seemed just as happy when she served and "ate" the food. This type of play continued through the sessions, but on the very last day she did something unusual. She began by making a "last supper" consisting of pie and ice cream. Her every movement seemed intentional and confident. Suddenly, she stopped in the middle of her play, announced that she did not want to cook any more, and decided to pretend that she was an artist. She painted me a flower, while remarking that she was the "boss" of her friends and of herself and that it felt happy to be the "boss." It seemed as if she had satiated her hunger for food and was thus able to pay attention to other interests. Our last activity together was to play the xylophone. Before we began to make music, she gave me instructions: "You can do it your way, I can do it my way, we've got to do it different ways, and make it sound like a song." There was harmony in our movements and in our music.

*Trust*

Trust is a basis for growth. Children need to feel they can count on those who take care of them. The children in the study, however, had all been abandoned in one way or another, passed to an orphanage, and from there to a new country. They tended to distrust adults and shield themselves from being hurt; to reveal themselves meant to become vulnerable.

Many parents have mentioned how their adopted children, especially in the weeks after arrival, would cling tightly and not allow the parents out of their sight. Min-sook's mother commented:

> To this day [3 years after the adoption] she will follow me around the house and if she discovers that I am not where she thinks I should be, she will walk in every room yelling "Mom, where are you?" She won't stop until she has found me. If I leave her and Steve [her brother] in the house while I run up to the bank, when I return she will be standing in the window.

Min-sook, in her "lost-child" plays, repeatedly acted out her distrust. She drew a series of picture stories on the blackboard and described the actions. In the first scene, a mother and her daughter go grocery shopping. In the next, the girl is crying in an open area, while her mother is shopping elsewhere. In the next, the mother promises to wait while the girl reluctantly leaves for the bathroom. When she returns, the mother has disappeared, and the girl is unable to find her. The child finds her way home alone, but she is unable to cook for herself, and eventually starves to death. The last scene of the series illustrates the funeral of the girl. The mother, in the background, is totally unconcerned. She has even forgotten the time of the funeral.

Soon-ja often played out the story of a mother who purposely deceives her child. One day, she took the role of a mother while pretending that I was her "baby." In a sweet voice, she promised "Honey, Momma's going to make your favorite dinner." Then she confided on the side, "Let's say I said I was making your favorite dinner but I didn't. I was making my favorite dinner. I tricked you." As the play went on, she again said, "See it was really my favorite dinner but you didn't know. Not 'til I put it on the table."

The issue of trust surfaced early in my relationship with Tae-ho. I had asked for his permission to include an observer in the next session. I had explained the observation room and its function. He clearly stated that he did not want to have anybody "looking at" him. He remarked that he felt "funny inside" when strangers looked at him. I respected his feelings and accepted his decision. However, he did not trust me. He asked me many "what if" questions, e.g., "What if the person has a separate key?" "What if the person comes in anyway?" I assured him that this would not happen without our permission. In the following session, he continuously looked at the one-way mirror, attempting to notice any movement, and finally asked to see the observation room. Of course, he did not find anybody there, as had been promised. This became an important turning point in our relationship.

I believe that as the children learned to trust me, they began to trust themselves, releasing some of their defenses, revealing their vulnerability and their strength. Young-hee's mother, at the end of the research project, reported to me:

> She always wanted to go with me wherever I went. Now she likes to go out and play with her friends. Before she wanted to stay home and have her friends come to her house. She has grown in so many ways.

Min-sook's mother gave a similar account:

> Not everything can be changed in a year but several changes have occurred that have made us very happy. Where she used to be afraid to stay alone, there are times now when she enjoys peace and quiet. Scared to speak in class, she now volunteers. Once unable to make the simplest decision, now she has no trouble expressing her wishes.

*Acceptance*

The children in my study went to excessive lengths to avoid disapproval and gain acceptance. They tended to be cautious and controlled. It was clear from the very first sessions that I needed to penetrate some of the barriers that kept them at a distance, not only from me but from their own emotions. I constantly encouraged them to express their feelings. Thanks in great measure to the play therapy process, most of the children overcame their extreme defensiveness and began to feel safe in verbalizing their feelings directly or acting them out, using the diverse materials in the room.

Many of the children displayed inordinate cleanliness and orderliness in their initial play. For example, Chol-soo was very careful to do everything "right." This meant not spilling a drop of water or dirtying his clothes. Even his voice was soft and even-toned. Min-sook was constantly asking, "What do you want me to do?," either directly or by seeking clues to the "right" behavior through my reactions. She took frequent inventories of what "bad" things the other children had done in the playroom. In a similar vein, Choon-ku detested broken toys. Once when he found a wheel which had fallen off a truck, he immediately defended himself—"I didn't do it"—and then went on to ask in angry voice, "Who broke the wheels off? Who broke the wheels off, huh?"

A common tendency was to avoid the display of any negative emotions. Young-il typically smiled when he felt insecure and began to giggle or laugh when the situation should have provoked anger. He seemed to believe that all negative emotions were "bad" and that he would be punished for exhibiting them. In later sessions, he confided how angry he was at his sister because she had called him names. It was clearly a great inner struggle to express himself on this matter. He kept repeating, "And don't tell anybody else. Don't tell my parents. This is just between you and I." Kyung-ai and Min-sook tended to put on empty, awkward smiles when they were upset. Behind this fear of showing their real feelings seemed to be the assumption, "If I show you how mad I can be, you won't like me, and you may send me away or back to Korea."

To an unusual degree, the children resorted to proper or conventional behavior to please others and avoid criticism. For Soon-ja, it was extremely important to stay out of trouble. On the day her mother had a conference with her teacher, she kept mentioning that some girls screamed in the bathroom and misbehaved but that she was not one of them, and never would be. Regarding her visit to a dentist, she described how she could obtain a prize from a nurse for being a "good girl," which meant not crying during the visit. From the way she described the episode, it was clear that acceptance as a "good girl" was even more important than the prize itself. In our sessions, when she felt accepted, her body relaxed and her play became noticeably more spontaneous.

## SYNTHESIS

At the core of the inner world of adopted Korean children lies an implicit sense of who they are. First and foremost, they know they are in a minority by virtue of being Korean and being adopted. They are like strangers in a strange land, trying to discern the landmarks and find their place. Their perceptions and understanding of the outer world are filtered through their sense of themselves. As they experience their being-in-the-world, this sense does not necessarily remain constant, but rather is affected by major currents of feelings and actions.

The meaning of being aliens in America was reflected in experiences at home, at school, and in their neighborhood. The children often became the object of severe, even humiliating teasing. They felt prejudice directed against them; feelings of alienation and rejection were apparent. To overcome these feelings, they attempted to demonstrate their identification with their new country. They "forgot" their native language and their memories from Korea. Speaking standard English was important to them as a symbol of acculturation, of being like other children. Their sense of themselves as Korean was gradually eroded. Contact with another Korean, such as myself, sometimes precipitated a crisis in this process of denial. It recalled their negative experiences in Korea and a fear that their previous life might be reenacted. Once this fear was overcome through reassurances as well as actual experiences with me, they gradually began to accept and identify with me, and thus, repossessed to some extent their Korean identity. Their sense of themselves as Korean in America became more integrated as evidenced in their frequent proclamations of being Korean Americans or American Koreans.

All the children in the study knew that they were born in Korea and had been adopted by their Caucasian families. The most important facet of adoption to the children was that they had their own mother and father. This implied a stable place in the world and a fulfillment of basic needs. On the other side was an excessive fear of losing their parents through various forms of separation. They viewed parents mostly in terms of the functions they performed. This view perhaps represented a need for absolute safety before making emotional investments in relationships with parents. While developing such relationships, they often referred to their past, particularly with reference to their biological parents. "Who carried me?" "Why did she not keep me?" "Why could she not keep me?" "Could they be alive?"—these were the constant probings. Since no definite answers could be given, the children developed elaborate fantasies to deal with these distressing questions.

Through adoption, the children gained not only parents but siblings as well. Their feelings toward other adopted Asian siblings in the family were notably close and protective. These feelings, however, did not exclude fighting or bickering. Those who gained other new siblings also expressed the nature of their relationship but without the closeness mentioned earlier.

For a few, becoming an American citizen initially confounded them. The cognitive and legal meaning of the occasion held little importance; the personal meaning of the event was more directly understood in terms of parental recognition and family celebration.

Just as their sense of self centered around feeling like strangers, so their most pressing needs related to this fact. These needs became apparent in their play, appearing as unsatisfied urges, unresolved issues, and frustrated drives that would surface in dramatic verbal and nonverbal activity. The most pronounced were needs for nurturance, trust, and acceptance.

The children displayed an inordinate need for food, as if this need had to be filled before there could be any major step forward. They repeatedly played out scenes in which they regressed to infancy and were rocked and bottle-fed. In other scenes, a deluge of make-believe food was conjured up and consumed.

A need for trust, especially in the form of stable human relationships which could be depended on, may have been increased by past disappointments as well as the obvious trauma of being uprooted. The children seemed to struggle with this problem. Their play indicated that trusting others often led to pain and disappointment, yet they seemed to yearn for genuine, trusting relationships. Only when they were convinced of constancy and dependability did they relax their defenses and begin to relate to others spontaneously. Until then, they constantly sought approval and acceptance by doing only the "right" or proper thing. When genuine acceptance became believable their sense of self was strengthened. They were able to pay attention to the development of spontaneous, free, and trusting interactions.

# 4. Birth Is More Than Once: Perspectives and Implications

My work suggests that birth is indeed possible more than once. The children who participated in my research project were all born to Korean parents in the Republic of Korea. For various reasons and under diverse circumstances, they were adopted into American families—a legal and symbolic re-birth. In my relationships with them, I witnessed them struggling through another birth—the birth of self. The sparkling laughter, creative exploration of limits and boundaries, the silences and confrontations, and the journey into fantasies made the texture of our shared lives rich and challenging.

## PERSPECTIVES AND IMPLICATIONS

Humanistic psychology attempts to integrate "various truth into the whole truth" (Maslow, 1968, p.viii), to supplement the observations of other orientations, and "to introduce further perspectives and insights" (Bugental, 1964, p.22). The task of this research was just that—to expand and supplement the observations of previous works in the field, making it more possible to arrive at the "whole truth." These perspectives and implications were derived from findings made available through the play therapy process; they offer insights into fuller understanding of the inner world of children adopted from Korea.

The first perspective revolves around the concept of survivors in a strange land. These children have been taken into a new culture without much preparation or awareness; suddenly, they have become outsiders. They exert considerable time and energy attempting to comprehend the rules of this strange environment and how they are supposed to be played. At first, they want to harmonize with their surroundings as unobtrusively as possible in order to minimize their alien traits. They are willing to adapt even at the expense of losing a feeling for their cultural background. They are willing, even eager, to suppress their feelings of loss, humiliation, isolation, and alienation. They harbor negative feelings but keep these feelings to themselves in order not to alienate others. They utilize a variety of coping mechanisms. They need ample evidence of sincerity before they allow themselves to trust others. It takes repeated assurances to convince them that it is permissable to display emotions. Slowly and gradually, they become comfortable in the new environment. The land is not too unusual any more, and they learn the intricacies and subtleties of the rules and language. In this process, the old self is eroded, a state of selflessness possesses them, and, if all goes well, a new self emerges.

This pespective implies several points. First, for those of us who work and live with these children, to understand the psychological state of the survivors, we need to feel empathy for these children and perceive the world from their point of view. A crucial factor is the recognition and appreciation of their feelings. This requires a particular dedication since these children tend to repress their feelings, especially the negative ones. Not only for our own understanding but for the mental health of the children themselves, it is imperative that we help them become aware of their emotions and find ways of expressing them. We can promote this by our own modeling as we share our inner lives with them and by communicating that it is quite acceptable to express one's feelings. Knowing that the suppression of "negative" emotions is related to their fear of "getting into trouble," we can offer reassurance. Then we can help them discover creative ways of owning their feelings and disclosing themselves for more authentic communicating and relating.

Further, we need to remember that the self-esteem of these children is closely related to how they view their physical and cultural differences. When they feel positive about themselves, they tend to view their differences as something of value. When the differences are seen in a negative light, they have negative effects on self-image and self-esteem. In order for these children to realize their potentials, a positive view of themselves is essential. Self-esteem grows internally through various experiences and relationships over a period of time. Parents should pay attention to these children's acute sensitivities and their need for positive reinforcement.

Jourard (1967) has stated that we reveal ourselves to those we have reason to trust. For the children to reveal themselves and their feelings to others, they need to feel a continuing trust. This was a consistent pattern in my interaction with them. The children's ability to trust is important in the kind of human relationships they develop. It took several months for many children in the study to establish an open and authentic relationship with me.

A genuine relationship is not a phenomenon that can be forced. To go beyond the superficial, functional stage of relating, and thereby invest oneself in an authentic relationship, involves the ability to trust others. To apply this in family situations, when children enter a family through adoption, the parents are usually ready, even eager, to endow the children with love, to take care of their needs, to protect them from dangers, and to impart their values. Because of the long adoptive waiting period, the parents have had ample time to prepare themselves for adoption. The children, however, have not had a similar preparation, and there is no reason for them to conclude that this family will be a permanent one. They may hope that it will be and they may try to behave in acceptable ways, but they also may use ingenious methods to test the family's commitment. During this process, if the children's experiences lead them to trust the family, their energy can be released into creative channels and they can build meaningful relationships.

The next perspective is a state of selflessness—a phase which the children must go through before they gain a solid sense of self. During this time, the "central core of the person" (Buhler & Allen, 1972, p.44) is weakly realized, and the need to conform to what is socially acceptable and to be approved is strong. The source of affirmation of self lies outside the person, who thereby allows others to shape his or her identity, and attempts to conform to other people's expectations. The children reveal a constant eagerness to please those around them by doing what they think is expected. They are trying to behave acceptably but at the expense of their individuality. In the state of selflessness, they rarely assert who they are and what they want. They are cautious in their moves, and quick to adjust to others' wishes. They are afraid of making mistakes, sometimes to the point of immobilization. This perspective offers an insight into the seemingly excessive need for approval among these children. I perceive this state of selflessness not as pathology but as a beginning point of a promising journey of self-growth.

To assist children to go through this phase successfully, it would be helpful for us to understand where their excessive need for approval and nurturing comes from. From the autobiographical data I have gathered, it appears that these needs arise from deficiencies in their pre-adoptive life as well as pressures to become assimilated. These needs are manifested in inappropriate behavior and in hidden messages. Some parents might feel anxious when their five-year-old son wants to drink out of a nursing bottle, crawl around babbling, or wear diapers. What I suggest is that before parents make a judgment, they might examine the behavior from the perspective of unmet needs. I have often heard adoptive parents express their concern about the seeming deficits in children's physical and psychological development as compared to American children of the same age. This lag in development and the accompanying aberrant behavior may be the adopted Korean child's way of striving to fulfill needs growing out of their special circumstances.

The last perspective concerns ethnicity. In trans-racial or trans-cultural adoption, an often discussed topic is how to assist children to keep their racial or cultural identity. From my experience as a Korean in America and from my research findings, it appears that there are considerable difficulties in maintaining the old culture while trying to adapt to the new one. Available energy is poured into exploring, coping, and experimenting. In this sense, the stronger the desire for acculturation, the faster is the erosion of one's cultural heritage.

There are five general stages children may go through before they are ready to reembrace their racial or cultural heritage. *The first is the stage of denial.* The children actively avoid and even refuse to acknowledge anything Korean—language, food, people, or customs. An example is the boy in the first chapter who puzzled his father by refusing to recognize anything Korean. This stage is marked by the children's intense desire to be bonded and be identified with their adoptive families. To overcome their feelings of alienation and rejection, they demonstrate their identification with the new country and family by denying or rejecting parts of themselves.

*The second stage is that of inner awakening.* As the children come to feel more comfortable in the new culture, they recognize, slowly and quietly, other Koreans as well as their own Korean heritage. They may show interest and pay attention to cultural objects and events, but in a passive way. This stage may not be noticeable to the parents or the children themselves, for it is more like an incubation period for what is to come.

*The third stage is acknowledgment.* This is a more noticeable and active stage than the second one. The children verbally admit and acknowledge their physical and cultural heritage in positive ways. An illustration of this stage is the description of Kyung-ai in Chapter 3, who recognized "many Koreans" at Marineland, who took delight in telling her parents about her observation. This active process of recognition and verbalization intensifies their experiences.

*The fourth stage, which is identification* begins from this point. The children look for other Koreans with whom to actively identify. They may be able to identify the similarities between themselves and other Koreans, and their differences from non-Koreans, the way Min-sook and Young-hee did in Chapter 3. Through these processes, the children often come to feel comfortable with their Korean identity; they learn to accept themselves as they are. When that happens, they may begin to find positive factors related to being Korean.

*The fifth stage, that of acceptance* entails a sense of equilibrium within themselves. Deeply buried memories may become available to the children, without undue prompting, and may come to a point of resolution when necessary. The sharing of these memories between the children and their parents can strengthen their link in the bonding process.

The stages presented here are guidelines to understanding the structure of the Korean child's world. While using them, I noted a great deal of variation in the small group with which I worked. Some children skipped a stage and others hardly progressed at all. However, it is now easier to understand such originally puzzling behavior as the children's violent reaction to me and the distress subsequent to exposure to Korean objects.

The presence of a Korean adult, the researcher, initially evoked fear in several children. They perceived me as a threat to their new life, afraid that I might take them back to Korea or adopt them myself, thereby removing them from their parents. This implies that it may not necessarily be helpful to introduce Korean adults into these children's lives before they are ready for such encounters. Many adoptive families with children beyond infancy (0 to 2 years) seek out their Korean friends, neighbors or acquaintances, hoping that the children will find solace in the company of other Koreans. I have seen this happen repeatedly in my capacity as a consultant to intercountry adoption programs. My findings, however, indicate that unless the children are ready, encountering a Korean adult may disrupt rather than assist their adjustment to the family.

When the help of a Korean is necessary, we need to keep

in mind and educate the Korean of the child's possible negative reaction. It is also imperative to prepare the children for the occasion, communicating as explicitely as possible what is to happen and who the people are. Initially, short and frequent visits with the parents present may be more comforting and reassuring to the children than prolonged ones. The children need to be reassured of no further major disruption in their lives. Through these experiences, the children can learn to trust their parents and feel safe to be with them. With this accomplished, more than half of the hurdles in the adjustment process will have been overcome.

Coming to terms with one's identity is an unending journey for many of us. Even those who have gone through the five stages successfully may find themselves struggling with the same or similar issues at different times and places in life. To facilitate the process of accepting their ethnic and cultural heritage, the children need, from their parents and other significant people in their lives, support, encouragement, understanding of, and respect for their inner feelings and dynamics. This process, in the long run, will help each child build a strengthened sense of self that will enable him or her to integrate the old and the new cultures.

# Epilogue

Adoption of Korean children into American families began in significant numbers only after the Korean War ended in 1953. Thousands of such children had been orphaned or abandoned, and Christian organizations offered their assistance as a humanitarian endeavor. The Korean War ended in 1953, yet these children continue to appear for adoption. Where do they come from? According to the 1977 Korean Statistical Year Book, only 11% of the children admitted to institutional facilities between 1969 and 1976 were orphans. Thirty percent were abandoned children. Little indication has appeared that the number of these children is decreasing as these abandoned children are those "without known parents" (Adams & Kim, 1971, p. 216). The reasons for abandonment are categorized (*Choong Ang Il Po*, February 17, 1981) in order of frequency: (1) unwed mothers and illegitimate births; (2) poverty or divorce; (3) orphans; (4) neglect by parents; and (5) legal loss of parental rights due to mental illness.

The availability of these children coincided with the desires of American families. In 1984, about 744 children from overseas were adopted by Michigan couples. About 88% of these children came from Korea (M. Hall, personal communication, June 26, 1985). These numbers provide a significant contrast to approximately 880 cases of domestic adoption in Michigan. In other words, taken as a whole, 40% of all children adopted by Michigan couples in 1984 were Korean! According to the statistics provided by Immigration and Naturalization Services, 7,322 children were adopted from abroad between October, 1982 and September, 1983. Among these, 4,635 were Korean children, that is, more than 60%. The following year during the same period, the number of Korean adoptions by American couples went up to 5,245.

Little attention has been paid to the phenomenon of Korean adoption in the professional literature. Research so far has consisted mainly of unpublished masters or doctoral theses, dealing with initial and long-term adjustment as judged by responses from adoptive parents. This book is written in an attempt to make the findings of my research readily available to all personnel who touch upon the lives of these children from Korea. As these children grow older, they often struggle with issues concerning their ethnic and cultural background, identity, self-esteem, in addition to all the other challenges every child faces in the process of growing up. Learning to live with the unknown about one's roots poses many difficulties. However, many of the questions asked about their background are unanswerable. Therefore, being able to accept the unknown and move forward, while difficult, is an essential task in their journey toward "wholeness."

Although the findings of my research were based on Korean children alone, my involvement as a consultant and a psychologist in this field has shown me that many issues discussed in this book are relevant to other foreign-born adopted children as well. Their ambivalent and fearful attitude toward people from the same country, their need to deal with prejudice, their perception of adoption, their feelings about themselves, and their psychological needs are so similar to the Korean children, that the name of another country could just as easily be substituted.

It is my deep desire that this book will ignite interest among academic centers, agencies, parent groups, and individuals to continue to discover knowledge about these children in a systematic way. The lack of research in the field has long been echoed. Now, more than any time before, with the increase of Korean children adopted by American families, it is critical that we promote better understanding about these children for the children themselves and for all of us who might facilitate their "re-birth."

# Bibliography

Adams, J., & Kim, H. B. A fresh look at intercountry adoptions. *Children.* 1971, *18,* 214-221.
Allen, F. *Psychotherapy with children.* New York: W. W. Norton, 1942.
Allport, G. *Becoming.* New Haven: Yale University Press, 1955.
Arons, M. Harari, C., & O'Donovan, D. Humanistic psychology: An overview. In F. Richards & I. Welch (Eds.), *Sightings: Essays in humanistic psychology.* San Francisco: Shields, 1973.
Axline, V. *Play Therapy.* New York: Ballantine, 1947.
Axline, V. *Dibs: In search of self.* Boston: Houghton Mifflin, 1964.
Baker, J. R. *Science and the planned state.* London: Macmillan, 1945.
Bridgman, P. W. *Reflections of a physicist.* New York: Philosophical Library, 1955.
Buck, P. *Children for adoption.* New York: Random House, 1964.
Bugental, J. F. T. The third force in psychology. *Journal of Humanistic Psychology.* Spring, 1964, *1*(4), 19-26.
Bugental, J. F. T. The challenge that is man. In J. F. T. Bugental (Ed.), *Challenges of humanistic psychology.* New York: McGraw-Hill, 1967.
Bugental, J. F. T. *The search for existential identity.* San Francisco: Jossey-Bass, 1976.
Buhler, C. Human life as a whole as a central subject of humanistic psychology. In J. F. T. Bugental (Ed.), *Challenges of humanistic psychology.* New York: McGraw-Hill, 1967.
Buhler, C., & Allen, M. *Introduction to humanistic psychology.* Belmont, Ca.: Wadsworth, 1972.

Cass, J. *Helping children grow through play.* New York: Schocken Books, 1971.

Chakerian, C. *Children of hope.* New York: Church World Services, 1966.

Chartrand, W. Application of selected components of a correspondence theory of cross-cultural adjustment to the adjustment of white families who have adopted older children from Korea (Doctoral dissertation, University of Minnesota, 1978). *Dissertation Abstracts International,* 1979, *39,* 9A (University Microfilm No. DEL 79-06295).

*Choong Ang Il Po (Choong Ang Daily Newspaper).* Seoul, Korea, February 17, 1981.

Clifton, P., & Ransom, J. An approach to working with the placed child. *Child Psychiatry and Human Development,* 1975, *6*(2), 107-117.

Colm, H. The self-defeating search for love. In C. Moustakas (Ed.), *The child's discovery of himself.* New York: Ballantine, 1975.

Combs, A., Richards, A., & Richards, F. *Perceptual psychology.* New York: Harper & Row, 1976.

Craig, P. E. The heart of the teacher: A heuristic study of the inner world of teaching (Doctoral dissertation, Boston University, 1978). *Dissertation Abstracts International,* 1978, *38,* 12A (University Microfilms No. 7808057).

Crane, P. S. *Korean patterns.* Seoul, Korea: Hollym, 1967.

deHartog, J. *The children.* New York: Atheneum, 1969.

DiVirgilio, L. Adjustment of foreign children in their adoptive homes. *Child Welfare.* 1956, *35* (9), 15-21.

Dorfman, E. Play Therapy. In C. R. Rogers (Ed.), *Client-centered therapy: Its current practice, implications and theory.* Boston: Houghton Mifflin, 1951.

Fedderson, M. D. An examination of the creative process emerging from the experience of a child in non-directive play therapy (Doctoral dissertation, University of Pittsburgh, 1975). *Dissertation Abstracts International,* 1975, *36,* 4B (University Microfilms No. 75-22439).

Frankl, V. E. *From death camp to existentialism.* Boston: Beacon Press, 1959.

Fromm, E. *Escape from freedom.* New York: Avon Books, 1965.

Gibran, K. *The prophet.* New York: Alfred A. Knopf, 1923.

Goble, F. *The third force.* New York; Grossman, 1970.

Granthem, R. J. Effects of counselor sex, race and language style on black students in initial interviews. *Journal of Counseling Pyschology,* 1973, *20,* 553-559.

Gross, K. *The play of man.* New York: Appleton, 1901.

Guilbault, C., & Guilbault, J. Abstract of a study: A descriptive study of the adjustment of Korean children adopted by families in Minnesota. In B. Kramer (Ed.), *The unbroken circle.* Minneapolis: Ours, 1975.

Hall, G. S. *Youth.* New York: Appleton, 1906.

Heidegger, M. *Existence and being.* South Bend, Ind.: Gateway, 1949.

Hobbs, N. Helping disturbed children: Psychological and ecological strategies. *American Psychologist.* 1966, *21,* 1105-1115.

Holt, B. *Outstretched arms.* 1972.

Husserl, E. *Ideas.* New York: Macmillan, 1962.

Jourard, S. M. Experimenter-subject dialogue: A paradigm for humanistic science of psychology. In J. F. T. Bugental (Ed.) *Challenges of humanistic psychology.* New York: McGraw-Hill, 1967.

Jourard, S. M. *The transparent self.* New York: Van Nostrand, 1971.

Keen, E. *A primer in phenomenological psychology.* New York: Holt, Rinehart & Winston, 1975.

Kelly, G. A. Humanistic methodology in psychological research. *Journal of Humanistic Psychology.* 1969, *11* (1), 53-65.

Keltie, P. *The adjustment of Korean children adopted by couples in the Chicago area.* Unpublished master's thesis, University of Illinois, 1969.

Kim, D. S. *Intercountry adoptions: A study of adolescent self-concept formation of Korean children who were adopted by American families.* Unpublished doctoral dissertation, University of Chicago. 1976.

Kim, H. T., & Reid, E. After a long journey. In B. Kramer (Ed.), *The unbroken circle*. Minneapolis: Ours, 1975.
Kramer, B. (Ed.). *The unbroken circle*. Minneapolis: Ours, 1975.
MacLeod, R. The phenomenological approach to social psychology. In A. E. Kuenzli (Ed.), *The phenomenological problem*. New York: Harper & Row, 1959.
Maslow, A. Self-actualizing people: A study of psychological health. In C. Moustakas (Ed.), *The self*. New York: Harper & Row, 1956.
Maslow, A. A philosophy of psychology: The need for a mature science of human nature. In F. Severin (Ed.), *Humanistic viewpoints in psychology*. New York: McGraw-Hill, 1965.
Maslow, A. *Toward a psychology of being*. New York: Van Nostrand, 1968.
Maslow, A. *The farther reaches of human nature*. New York: Penguin Books, 1971.
May, R. (Ed.). *Existence*. New York: Basic Books, 1958.
May, R. *Psychology and the human dilemma*. New York: Van Nostrand, 1967.
May, R. Relation of existential to humanistic psychology. In A. Sutich & M. Vich (Eds.), *Readings in humanistic psychology*. New York: Free Press, 1969.
McNamara, J. *The adoption advisor*. New York: Hawthorn Books, 1975.
Mech, E. Trends in adoption research. In *Perspectives on adoption research*. New York: Child Welfare League of America, 1965.
Miller, H. *Korea's international children*. New York: Lutheran Social Welfare Conference of America, 1971.
Miller, W. R. *Short footsteps on a long journey: The poetry of Chan Sei Ghow*. St. Louis: Fokestone Press, 1967.
Moustakas, C. *Children in play therapy*. New York: McGraw-Hill, 1953.
Moustakas, C. True experience and the self. In C. Moustakas (Ed.), *The self*. New York: Harper & Row, 1956.
Moustakas, C. *Loneliness*. Englewood Cliffs, N.J.: Prentice Hall, 1961.

Moustakas, C. (Ed.). *The child's discovery of himself.* New York: Ballantine, 1966.

Moustakas, C. *Creativity and conformity.* New York: Van Nostrand, 1967.

Moustakas, C. Heuristic research. In J. F. T. Bugental (Ed.), *Challenges of humanistic psychology.* New York: McGraw-Hill, 1967.

Moustakas, C. *Individuality and encounter.* Cambridge, England: Doyle, 1968.

Moustakas, C. *Psychotherapy with children: The living relationship.* New York: Ballantine, 1970.

Moustakas, C. *Touch of loneliness.* Englewood Cliffs, N.J.: Prentice Hall, 1975.

National Bureau of Statistics/Economic Planning Board. *Korea statistical year book.* (24), Seoul, Korea, November, 1977.

*New York Times Magazine. Partnership: Republic of Korea-United States.* July 15, 1979, 45-71.

Nogaard, H. The placement and adjustment of children from Korea in Minnesota schools. In B. Kramer (Ed.), *The unbroken circle.* Minneapolis: Ours, 1975.

O'Conner, L., Jr. *The adjustment of a group of Korean and Korean-American children adopted by couples in the United States.* Unpublished master's thesis, University of Tennessee, 1964.

Piaget, J. *Play, dreams and imitation in childhood* (C. Gattegno & F. M. Hodgson, trans.). New York: W. W. Norton, 1962.

Polanyi, M. *Personal knowledge: Towards a post-critical philosophy.* Chicago: University of Chicago Press, 1958.

Polanyi, M. *Science, faith, and society.* Chicago: University of Chicago Press, 1964.

Polanyi, M. *The tacit dimension.* Garden City, N.Y.: Doubleday, 1967.

Polya, G. *How to solve it: A new aspect of mathematical method.* Princeton: Princeton University Press, 1945.

Pu, C. H. *Adoption and child welfare: Towards domestic adoption.* Seoul, Korea: Holt Children's Services, 1978 (Korean text).

Rank, O. *Will therapy.* New York: Alfred A. Knopf, 1936.
Rhodes, W. C. The disturbing child: A problem of ecological management. *Exceptional Children.* 1967, *33,* 449-455.
Rogers, C. R. *Counseling and psychotherapy: Newer concepts in practice.* Boston: Houghton Mifflin, 1942.
Rogers, C. R. On our science of man. In W. Coulson & C. R. Rogers (Eds.), *Man and the science of man.* Columbus, Ohio: Merrill, 1968.
Rogers, C. R. *Freedom to learn.* Columbus, Ohio: Merrill, 1969.
Rogers, C. R. Toward a science of the person. In A. Sutich & M. Vich (Eds.), *Readings in humanistic psychology.* New York: Free Press, 1969.
Rogers, C. R. Some thoughts regarding the current philosophy of the behavioral sciences. In D. Schultz (Ed.), *The Science of psychology: Critical reflections.* New York: Appleton-Century-Crofts, 1970.
Rosenberg, A. *The adoption of Oriental children by Caucasian-American parents.* Unpublished master's thesis, University of Wisconsin, 1968.
Schaefer, C. (Ed.). *The therapeutic use of child's play.* New York: Jason Aronson, 1976.
Singer, J. *The child's world of make-believe: Experimental studies of imaginative play.* New York: Academic Press, 1973.
Spiegelberg, H. The essence of phenomenological methods. In H. Spiegelberg (Ed.), *The phenomenological movement.* Vol. 2. The Hague: Martinus Nyhoff, 1965.
Sullivan, H. S. *The psychiatric interview.* New York: W. W. Norton, 1954.
Sutich, A., & Vich, M. (Eds). *Readings in humanistic psychology.* New York: Free Press, 1969.
Suzuki, D. T. *The field of Zen.* New York: Harper & Row, 1970.
Taft, J. *Otto Rank: A biographical study based on notebooks, letters, collected writings, therapeutic achievements and personal associations.* New York: Julian Press, 1958.

Tillich, P. *The courage to be.* New Haven: Yale University Press, 1952.

Toussieng, P. Realizing the potential in adoption. *Child Welfare.* 1971, *50,* 322-327.

Valk, M. *Korean-American children in American adoptive homes.* New York: Child Welfare League of America, 1957.

Van Kaam, A. *Existential foundations of psychology.* Vol. 3, Pittsburgh: Duquesne University Press, 1966.

Walder, R. Psychoanalytic theory of play. In C. Schaefer (Eds.), *The therapeutic use of child's play.* New York: Jason Aronson, 1976.

Welwood, J. Exploring mind: Form, emptiness and beyond. *Jounal of Transpersonal Psychology.* 1976, *2,* 89-99.

Will, O. Introduction. In H. S. Sullivan, *The psychiatric interview.* New York: W. W. Norton, 1954.

Wood, J. *A study of the long-term adjustment of children of Korean heritage adopted by American families.* Unpublished doctoral dissertation, University of Oregon, 1972.

*Yearbook of public health and social statistics.* Seoul, Korea: Ministry of Public Information, 1965.

## COURTESY ORDER FORM

Please send me _____ copies of *Birth Is More Than Once* at $7.95 each.     $_____

**SPECIAL**
On orders of 5 or more you may deduct $1.00 per book.     _____

On orders of 25 or more you may deduct $1.50 per book.     _____

Michigan residents please add 4% tax.     _____

Postage and Handling, $1.50 for the first copy. Please add $0.50 for each additional copy.     _____

**TOTAL AMOUNT DUE**     $_____

PAYMENT IN U.S. FUNDS MUST ACCOMPANY ORDER. Please make check payable and send orders to:

    **SUNRISE VENTURES**
    708 Parkman Drive
    Bloomfield Hills, MI 48013

Name _____
                 (Please Print)

Address _____

City _____ State _____ Zip _____

**IRONCLAD GUARANTEE:** If you find this book unsuitable for any reason, you may return it within 10 days in saleable condition for a full refund.

## COURTESY ORDER FORM

Please send me _____ copies of *Birth Is More Than Once* at $7.95 each.     $_____

**SPECIAL**

On orders of 5 or more you may deduct $1.00 per book.     _____

On orders of 25 or more you may deduct $1.50 per book.     _____

Michigan residents please add 4% tax.     _____

Postage and Handling, $1.50 for the first copy. Please add $0.50 for each additional copy.     _____

**TOTAL AMOUNT DUE**     $_____

PAYMENT IN U.S. FUNDS MUST ACCOMPANY ORDER. Please make check payable and send orders to:

**SUNRISE VENTURES**
708 Parkman Drive
Bloomfield Hills, MI 48013

Name _____
(Please Print)

Address _____

City _____ State _____ Zip _____

**IRONCLAD GUARANTEE**: If you find this book unsuitable for any reason, you may return it within 10 days in saleable condition for a full refund.